AF393121

The Way
A Path to Nowhere

Ilyas El-Amin

Good Trade Books

© 2026 GOOD TRADE BOOKS

All rights reserved.

No part of this publication may be reproduced,

stored in a retrieval system, or transmitted

in any form or by any means without the prior

written permission of the publisher.

Published by

GOOD TRADE BOOKS

Author

Ilyas El-Amin

ISBN: 978-1-972045-05-3

First Edition

Printed in the United States of America

To the believers, keep your hearts open to hear the whispers of guidance towards truth and understanding.

To the dreamers, seekers, and wanderers along the path may your visions of tomorrow be replaced with the patience of living today.

Dylan, stay curious. Humbly walking the path that life unfolds before your feet allowing gratitude to be your compass.

The Opening In the name of The Most Merciful, The Most Compassionate. In the name of The One God that binds us all. There is only The One God. There is One Way for us all and it is the way of submission. The things that I will share are nothing new. There's no new information that a more eloquent teacher hasn't already said. There's no new revelation, we have the Prophets (peace be upon them all) for that. This, at best, is a book to help us all remember. If I have written anything that is incorrect, please forgive my ignorance. If you read anything that you find significant or true it is truly a miracle and attributable only to The One God. May peace be upon you.

Do what thou will with me Allah, for I know that I am a lover of you, and you are a lover of me; never shall we harm the other. Give abundantly to those that have yet to empty themselves of themselves. Allow the abundance of your giving to swell their bellies making space for you to abide. Awaken within me servitude, to help those that have yet to realize that there is nothing that is needed. Help my eyes to see that it is only you and I, my God; for you exist in everyone I meet. Continue unraveling the mystery of me so that I may fully know you. Forgive me my inadequacies and set my feet solely in the pathway of your mercy, for your mercy prevails over your wrath. Thank you for giving me the understanding that the worst of all inequities and the easiest to relieve is knowledge.

~Ilyas

The Purpose

The goal of this book is to help us to remember, first that there is a way that leads to our fulfillment and secondly to remind us that walking this path is our soul's yearning and the only thing that will satisfy the ache within us all for freedom. We collectively desperately need to rediscover ourselves so that we can fully engage with this life and touch True Reality and Peace. We can no longer slumber in the hope that our sorrows will one day magically disappear. Our suffering is interconnected, and we each must make the effort to resign our individual suffering and start to create a better world.

Throughout this writing, I use the name Allah rather than God. I do this because linguistically, this is how I understand The One to be: Allah is more accurate than God. Although these words mean the same, in the English language, God can be attached to many other prefixes and suffixes which drastically change the meaning of the supremely divine nature of what we mean when referring to The Source of all things. Whereas the Arabic word Allah is singular and translates most accurately as The God. The God that exists above all things and all understanding.

Part I

The Path

There exists a path that eludes definition, known only through experience. Attempts to name it have led to the emergence of competing religions, each asserting itself as the singular truth. This fundamental misunderstanding has precipitated wars and violence, as factions vie for dominance over one another. The genuine path lies in the act of submission—to the singular truth of our origins and our interconnectedness. This journey fosters wisdom and understanding, attainable only through a commitment to peace and enduring compassion for ourselves and those around us. Every messenger and prophet of True Reality has imparted this lesson, regardless of the rituals or traditions from which they hailed. Indeed, the world around us instructs us through every living entity. Yet, we have neglected to observe, closing our eyes to Reality in favor of convenience and luxury. Our blindness has rendered us incapable of trusting our steps or the path ahead, plunging us into a state of confusion that often manifests as fear and hysteria. We resemble the figures in Plato's allegory of the cave—individuals deprived of light and confined to shadows, unable to grasp True Reality and only capable of perceiving fragments of our own creation.

At some juncture, we collectively chose to overlook the essence of our being in pursuit of an idealized self. We forsook the miraculous in favor of the mundane, abandoning our communal identity even as our population grew. As a species, we are more interconnected than ever before; paradoxically, the gulf between us has never been wider. We have estranged ourselves from one another and from our own selves, clinging to the misguided belief that tomorrow will be better than today. Thus, we wait. Some await a savior, others anticipate an end—whether personal or collective. Some yearn for happiness to be bestowed upon them, while others simply wait without purpose. Many seek enlightenment and self-improvement, hoping for external change. We find ourselves in a state of inaction, distracting ourselves with the illusion of living. We perpetuate paradoxes, aware that there is truly nothing to accomplish; we are here, and what is required of us is to understand our individual identities and how we relate to every other being in existence. Yet, we have forsaken this straightforward task in favor of prioritizing comfort and ease above all else.

We recognize this truth reflected in every aspect of our world, shaped by our own hands. Everything we engage in is a product of our own choices. At any moment, we can decide to stop and acknowledge that nothing is lacking. There is nothing to fix or battle against. The foundation of our existence is that there is simply nothing until we choose differently. If you find dissatisfaction in your job, change it. If you are unhappy with your existence, alter it. We possess the ability to change whatever causes us suffering or obstructs our reconnection with ourselves and the world around us. The adage that "99% of life is merely showing up" holds true. We are present; the question remains: what comes next? We can continue to pursue futile endeavors aimed at accumulating wealth and comfort, but as we approach death, what will become of the wealth and comfort we so ardently sought? Did our pursuits hold any significance? Did they cultivate peace, happiness, and joy for ourselves or others?

Our existence is intrinsically intertwined with an unknown force and with one another. It is through our collective voices and narratives that we co-create every facet of our reality. This underscores the importance of each individual story and perspective. To disregard any part of this narrative is to disconnect from the truth of our shared experience.

For this understanding to be fully realized, we must acknowledge that all stories contain fallacies. Any written text, regardless of its perceived sanctity, cannot encompass the entirety of truth; it can only point toward it. Recognizing the imperfections inherent in these representations does not diminish the perfection of truth itself.

We must refrain from elevating the created above the creator and instead learn to view the created as a reflection of the creator. This perspective is essential for gaining insight into the profound nature of existence. This foundational principle is echoed in the Christian Bible, which states that "the letter kills, but the Spirit gives life." Similarly, Gautama's flower sermon illustrates this concept, and it resonates across various religious teachings.

Regrettably, the infinite reality of any observed entity is often reduced to a finite understanding, constrained by the observer's limited experience and comprehension. Consequently, our inability to perceive reality beyond our labels leads to a superficial understanding: the letter remains merely a letter, and the flower is simply a plant.

In the Qur'an, the narrative of humanity's creation reveals that Allah taught Adam the names of the animals. Before this naming, did these creatures possess identities, or were they merely creations of the creator? Does a dog perceive itself merely as "dog"? We assign attributes to defined objects, and through our labels, we view them solely through those attributions. Their existence becomes contingent upon our limited perception.

Our conflicts stem from this fundamental flaw in reasoning: the misconception that perceived truth equates to ultimate truth. This grave error has hindered our collective evolution. Until we accept that our individual experiences do not hold superiority over others' understandings, we risk perpetuating misguided totalitarianism and divisive, manmade doctrines.

(By the passage of time. Surely humanity is in grave loss. Except those who have believed and done righteous deeds, and advised each other to truth and advised each other to patience.) Holy Quran, Surah 103, Al-'Asr

In the beginning, there was nothing and from that nothingness emerged something. That is something that every one of us can agree upon, regardless of any of our belief systems or ideations. For some, this phenomenon is explained and understood scientifically, while others explain and understand this moment mystically or spiritually. The moment is further broken down within these two dominant religions. Within the scientific community, numerous hypotheses are used to explain how everything began, some even conflict with one another. Amongst the spiritual traditions, we also see a variety of conflicting teachings that explain our beginning. Despite all the nuances of the different ways to look at our shared starting point, it all comes back to the notion that from nothing emerged something, and that something became us.

I do not claim to be a scientist, nor will I attempt to explicate the intricacies of connecting with ourselves or with one another through the framework of any specific religion. My life has been devoted to the pursuit of Truth, with spirituality serving as my primary tool for exploration. Throughout my journey, I have encountered various spiritual traditions, each of which has presented a common challenge: the presence of other people. Our spiritual practices often feel unfulfilling because we tend to rely on others to connect us with Allah and with Truth. Many have distanced themselves from the teachings in our holy texts, feeling unfulfilled, betrayed, or even abused by those they trusted to guide them toward Allah. I empathize with the frustration that can lead one to forsake spiritual understanding. Indeed, I concur that our spiritual traditions frequently fall short. However, what relevance does this have to Allah? How does human fallibility affect the perfection of Allah and the essence of True Reality? What benefit is there in abandoning Allah for the sake of comfort when suffering persists regardless?

To every people, Allah has imparted an understanding of His nature and the origins of our existence. Although these understandings may not seem harmonious at first glance, a deeper reflection reveals their interconnectedness. They are narrating a singular story, originating from the same source: Allah. Since the dawn of creation, our collective consciousness has sought to comprehend the nature of our existence. Consequently, irrespective of the cultures or traditions that have emerged, we share essential truths. Just as "blue" is universally recognized, despite the varying languages that define it, the words we use to describe Allah, the universe, and existence may differ, yet they all point to the same indescribable force that binds us.

Unfortunately, we have become so focused on our individual perspectives and traditions that we mistake them for the entirety of divine understanding. We have lost sight of Allah in favor of our rituals, believing that adherence to tradition equates to a commitment to Allah. However, traditions can only guide us to the threshold of the path; they cannot encompass the path itself. Our connection to Allah cannot be fully contained within texts, as Allah transcends what can be physically grasped. It is misguided to assert ownership over the Creator of all that is known and unknown. Continuing down this path leads us to a state of collective blindness. Yet, this need not be our fate. We have the capacity to transcend our limitations and evolve, achieved through the humble act of relinquishing our arrogance in favor of submission—to the singular truth that we are all inadequate and distant from The Truth.

Our shared experiences offer the only avenue to fully comprehend our identities and our relationship with Allah. While I acknowledge that our sacred texts elaborate on our shared reality, individual interpretations inevitably differ. We have allowed arrogance and pride to dictate our faith, leading us to follow blindly stubbornly defending against what appears different. The believers of faith, hope, and Allah are divided into sects, separated by dogmatism. Separated by egoism. Separated by dualism. But the family of believers are just that—a family—and cannot continue to fight amongst ourselves about who has the "truth." There is only One, one Allah, one Truth, and throughout the years there have been many who have taught their communities the simple truth of pure monotheism.

These teachers, messengers, and prophets guided their communities through various rituals and methods to comprehend and connect with the singular source of creation. While their messages may differ in expression, they fundamentally convey the same truth.

Truth is constant and immutable—much like the equation $2 + 2 = 4$, a fact universally acknowledged. Yet, there are countless alternative equations that also yield the answer of four, such as $1 + 3$, $4 + 0$, $5 - 1$, and even $1 + 1 + 1 + 1$. This illustrates that there are infinite paths to the same conclusion, each valid in its own right.

In contrast, religion often lacks this perspective; many adherents cling to their belief systems as the sole pathway to truth. This rigidity can lead to conflict, even war, over which interpretation is correct. If the ultimate truth remains unchanged, it is both trivial and immature to engage in disputes over the differing methodologies.

(To every community We sent a messenger: "Worship Allah and avoid idolatry." Some of them Allah guided, while others deserved misguidance. So, travel through the earth, and see what the fate of the deniers was.)

~Holy Quran Surah an-Nahl ayah 36

(We have appointed a law and a practice for every one of you. Had Allah willed, He would have made you a single community, but He wanted to test you regarding what has come to you. So compete with each other in doing good. Every one of you will return to Allah and He will inform you regarding the things about which you differed.)

~ Holy Qur'an Surah al-Ma'ida ayah 48

(When it is said to them: 'Follow what Allah hath revealed'. They say: 'Nay we shall follow the ways of our fathers'. What! Even though their fathers were void of wisdom and guidance?")

~Holy Quran surah al-Baqarah ayah 170

As a species and society, we are evolving, and as we are working to evolve beyond infancy it is time to allow the ego to dim. It is time that we stop fighting one another over that about which we have little understanding. The majority of people in the world have blindly followed other humans and never sought to experience or understand themselves, life, one another, or Allah. We are at a loss as to what exactly it is that we believe. Most of us believe, for example, that Allah is a he: but Allah is not he nor she. Allah cannot be perceived by human terms. Allah cannot be understood by human identities and parallelisms. Allah cannot be compiled into a book of 66 chapters, or 114 or even two million: to reduce something that is infinite to a finite object and proclaim that you hold the entirety of understanding is like taking a glass and filling it with ocean water and then proclaiming that you have the entire world's ocean in your hand— and, further still, discounting anyone else that has dipped their cup into the same ocean as a blasphemer and liar when they also profess to hold the ocean within their hand. These are the actions of a child, an unlearned individual who has not taken the time to ponder their own reality and limitations.

(When I was a child, I spoke as a child, I understood as a child, I thought as a child: but when I became a man, I put away childish things.)

~Holy Bible I Corinthians 13:11

We inhabit a time in which our messengers are often revered and celebrated beyond the essence of their messages, leading us to rely on others to connect us with Allah and the ultimate Truth. As human beings, we find it challenging to engage with or comprehend anything that eludes our tangible senses. We require the ability to touch, see, and feel in order to accept concepts and integrate them into our reality. Our senses anchor our experiences, rendering us somewhat enslaved by them; thus, ideas that transcend our physical perception appear unattainable.

In this context, we have diminished our capacity to trust in our instinctual and spiritual intelligence, resulting in a disconnection from true fulfillment—Allah. For Allah embodies the essence of every moment, and genuine reality is accessible only in the present. Many religions affirm this notion, yet it is often linked to doctrines of prosperity in both the physical and spiritual realms. Consequently, endeavors to embrace this principle are frequently undermined by a misguided belief that extraordinary experiences are indicators of success and fulfillment.

In reality, encountering Allah and experiencing the present moment can initially seem quite ordinary or mundane. We must learn to appreciate that simplicity does not equate to a lack of depth. By shifting our perspective, we can uncover the nuanced beauty hidden within the mundane. When we begin to recognize the miraculous in our everyday lives, we can break free from the constraining mindset of victimhood—a belief that life is happening to us unfairly, depriving us of our desired outcomes.

Even more concerning is the sense of despair that arises from the belief that we are doomed to a life of misery. Our perceived successes and failures are not governed by fatalism. Such an ideology suggests a partiality from Allah, which is fundamentally untrue. Allah is Al-Wadud and Al-'Adl, The Loving and The Just. Each of us is equally afforded the opportunity to engage with life symbiotically and cultivate gratitude. Life unfolds not merely because it is destined to do so, but simply because it is.

Can you discern the distinction?

The subtle difference between these two perspectives highlights the contrast between peace and suffering. Our purpose in this life is to learn how to emerge from our self-imposed cocoon of suffering and embrace the freedom that comes with peace and gratitude.

My unraveling

Who am I? Who am I, that I should be writing anything concerning religion, Spirituality, science, or anything for that matter? To save anyone who may be reading these words the time, I openly declare that I am a fool. I have no qualifications. I have not labored through years of study that qualify me to speak upon anything and be labeled as an expert. I, like the majority of the world, am moving through life one moment at a time, trying to make sense of things. Spiritually, I consider myself to be Muslim, although I have and occasionally do participate in numerous spiritual traditions.

A Muslim, in its simplest definition, is an individual who submits to Allah within the framework of Islam. More broadly, a Muslim is someone committed to establishing peace. This concept resonates with me as both attainable and visible in every moment of life. It has become a guiding principle for my interactions with the world around me. When conflicts arise with friends, family, or colleagues, I pause to reflect: "Are my words, actions, intentions, and desires aligned with peace?" If not, I consider what steps might foster harmony in the situation and what within me may be obstructing a peaceful interaction. I ask myself how my partner and I can achieve peace in that moment.

I strive to avoid the popular cultural notion of peace as a utopia. Peace does not always manifest as tranquility, either internally or externally. According to the Holy Bible, Jesus teaches that sometimes the path to peace may involve conflict. Such conflict can serve as a catalyst for love and understanding, provided it is approached with compassion.

The Qur'an reminds us that Allah does not favor the aggressor. Conflicts will inevitably arise among us, and it is essential to remember that peace is the ultimate goal of every disagreement. This practice demands effort and represents a struggle against our innate desire to "win." It is a sacred struggle against the self, a journey that each of us undertakes throughout our lives. The objective is to consciously engage in this process, ultimately reaping the rewards of our efforts. The moment of acceptance of these rewards varies for each individual; for some, it may occur early in life, while for others, it may come later. Nevertheless, we all experience this moment, culminating in the understanding of fundamental questions: Who am I, and why am I here? These questions are imprinted on our souls, and throughout our lives, we endeavor to either discover or evade the profundity of both the questions and their answers.

It was during a meditation session that I first encountered nothingness—an experience devoid of self, of others, and of the world. I was profoundly shaken as I became one with the void. I had anticipated a range of experiences, yet all that emerged was sheer nothingness, which I was unprepared for. I expected to feel, see, or understand something, to hear something profound. In that moment, I would have claimed to have no expectations, but that would have been disingenuous; I certainly anticipated some form of occurrence. Prior to that moment, much had transpired, yet ultimately, it led to nothingness. I struggle to articulate what nothingness felt like, or how I recognized its existence in the absence of self. Yet it was undeniably present, and I grasped its reality. I cannot explain how it came to be or how it dissipated; I only know that the instant I identified and labeled the nothingness, it vanished, replaced by my breath. It simply existed, and in the wake of that moment, I was inundated with questions: Was I dreaming? Was I asleep? Did I experience a near-death phenomenon? Is this what meditation entails? Do others undergo similar experiences? As I navigated these inquiries, I realized the vastness of what lies beyond my comprehension. I had to accept that this moment was just that—a moment —and attempting to understand it is akin to trying to define a single breath.

I mention this experience for those who hold the belief that death is the end. If this was a fleeting glimpse of death, then there is undoubtedly something beyond. The nothingness I encountered was profound. I believe that the inevitability of death parallels the inevitability of life; both occur, along with the myriad moments that transpire between these two events. One undeniable truth is that nothing is permanent; all things continue to evolve, perhaps even death itself.

The earth is a mirror of our relationship to Allah. As the earth grows grass and trees so too does Allah grow people. This is the reality of our collective experience. Within each of us is a piece of Allah, for Allah is nearer to you than your jugular vein (Surah Qaf 50:16). The only thing that separates us from Allah is our minds. It is the veil that keeps Allah hidden from our view. Practicing meditation can help with getting into a state of being that will allow us to perceive Allah throughout our consciousness and life experience. In meditation we can learn to hear the higher vibrations of the mind and recognize that as our nearest connection to Allah. As we develop our ability to experience a meditative state, following and hearing that guiding voice among the millions that populate the mind, we begin the pathway towards enlightenment. This pathway is our birth right as well as the only possible path since we are here only for the purpose of experiencing ourselves and understanding our connection to Allah. There is nothing else to do. There is no other choice. Sure, we are able to distract ourselves with a multitude of other things all throughout life. The problem is none of them are actually a distraction and only further show us who we are and what we believe to be the nature of our relationship with Allah. That is the way.

We came into this world with a pure connection to love and it was easy. We didn't need rules or instructions to know that we were connected, we just were. We wanted everyone to have their heart's desire. As children if we saw someone suffering, we wanted to empathize with them and to try to end the suffering. We knew without a shadow of a doubt that everyone in our lives mattered and directly impacted our well- being. These are things that we knew without instruction, without ritual: and then we begin to learn what our societies deemed as necessary. At some point our ancestors begin to learn that the fear of "others" is the key to our survival and even progress. We continue in their tradition and thus our villages have been diminished to single households and everyone outside of our new village walls is susceptible to suspicion. Our suspicious nature becomes multiplied throughout cities, nations, and countries as we look to the greater other as an enemy and therefore a deceiver of the truth, our truth.

We can only overcome our collective fear-based suspicion by abandoning our individual addiction to fear. Fear exists in a dreamlike state enticing us to live our lives of fantasy, dominated by egoic desires. Working to eradicate our ego by diminishing our desires to our base needs creates the necessary space to remove the fear and suspicion of the other. We start to balance the scales understanding that we don't have to hoard resources in order to sustain ourselves. This is the beginning step towards creating a more equitable society.

The worst of all inequities and the easiest to relieve is knowledge. There is a way of deep knowing within each of us. Some of us have an easier time remembering the pure truth of our collective origins and to keep that knowledge of interconnectivity from one another can be equated to the peril of the rich man that Jesus depicted as missing the gates of heaven. Our societies historically have been corrupted because of this type of inequity. Those that hold knowledge, hold power and the knowledgeable have often actively pursued to keep others in a state of ignorance to follow blindly.

(Read: In the Name of your Lord who created. Created man from a clot. Read: And your Lord is the Most Generous. He who taught by the pen. Taught man what he never knew.)
~Al Quran Surah al-Alaq ayats 1-5

(Say, ˹O Prophet,˺ "Are those who know equal to those who do not know?" None will be mindful ˹of this˺ except people of reason.)
~Al Quran Surah az-Zumar, Ayah 9

I choose to place my trust in Allah and the creations of Allah over the constructs of humankind. We have allowed faith to be supplanted by fear, which permeates every aspect of our lives. We have become captivated by darkness, drawing incessantly from the well of fear, resulting in a world steeped in anxiety—the poison of our existence. Society has led us to believe that we are surrounded by adversaries, yet the most significant enemy we face resides within ourselves. Distanced from love, we have forgotten its essence, leading us to perceive ourselves as isolated individuals. Our fears dictate our lives, blinding us to the truth that we are never truly alone.

Despite the lessons fear may impart, within each of us resides a fragment of the universe. We are beings of energy, a concept well-articulated by Einstein's theory of relativity: $E=mc^2$. This equation illustrates the interchangeability of energy and mass, allowing us to quantify our mass, which corresponds to the energy we embody. Our bodies, referred to as such because they contain something, house our consciousness or soul. Essentially, our physical form encapsulates our true essence. The thin barrier of skin separates our invisible selves from the broader creation, yet it does not fully isolate us; our bodies are porous and influenced by our environment at the microscopic level. We exist as part of our surroundings while simultaneously attempting to escape from them—including from ourselves. We cloak ourselves in anxieties about an uncertain future and the remnants of the past. This inability to remain present manifests as physical ailments, such as pain and depression. We find ourselves in a perpetual state of fear—haunted by the "what ifs" that have plagued us since childhood.

Amidst this turmoil, a gentle voice persists, whispering, "Don't be afraid; it's okay; you're not alone." This voice reiterates these simple yet profound words, urging us to listen. He who has ears, let him hear.

(The believers are but a single brotherhood: So make peace and reconciliation between your two (contending) brothers; and fear Allah, that ye may receive Mercy.)
~Al Quran Surah Al-Hujuraat, Ayah 10

The Way

There is a way within each of us that points toward the way Home. We spend our entire lives are either looking for or running away from heaven, Allah—from that place at our core that feels safe. We know that it's our right, and we know that it is always going to loom there, nagging at us, begging for us to listen. Yet instead of turning towards it, we muffle the voice with television and cellphones. We ignore that part of us that begs for us to sit down and heal what is broken and to embrace our natural right to be in a state of peace.

When we begin to engage in the peace process, we initiate a healing of aspects within ourselves that have long been neglected. These neglected areas often manifest as diseases or illnesses in both our bodies and consciousness. The essence of disease or illness lies in the understanding that our experiences are not dictated by external factors; rather, nothing outside of us establishes our internal realities. Our inner worlds collectively shape our outer existence.

This concept is most easily illustrated through the reproductive process of birth. That which exists internally ultimately manifests externally at birth. A child emerges as a product of initial emotions and thoughts, followed by internal substances that coalesce into a physical being. This principle applies universally to everything we observe in our world today: we are products of our internal dimensions. Yet, we often perceive our inner worlds as either nonexistent or inconsequential to our external reality. We tend to assign value solely to the physical realm, dismissing anything beyond our physical senses as mere figments of imagination. Society has established entire disciplines focused exclusively on the physical world, neglecting the inner dimensions of self. In doing so, we have often abandoned our connection to Allah and spirituality, deeming the outer expressions of our spiritual beliefs flawed.

Our religions have frequently let us down because we sought intercessory experiences between ourselves and Allah; in essence, we looked outward for guidance to navigate our inner dimensions. We relied on others to dictate our beliefs and practices. The moment we turn outside ourselves for solutions to our inner struggles, we set ourselves on a path of potential misguidance. Each of us occupies the same position in relation to Allah; there is no one greater than another in this world. No one can claim to have seen beyond this life to elucidate what lies ahead, nor can anyone truly delve into the depths of another individual's being to reveal what is concealed. This task is inherently impossible. We are all bound by the limitations of our understanding and individually tasked with the mission of demystifying our experiences. This is the path forward.

This understanding is the essence of existence and the price we must each pay for a life free of suffering. It is insufficient to merely occupy a church pew and recite the words of another; repeating holy scriptures from memory offers only a temporary solace to a profound wound. While the journey of healing may begin in such spaces, it cannot end there. Our reliance on the experiences of others to explain our own existence has led to disenchantment with religion and spirituality. We have often neglected to personalize the teachings of those who have successfully navigated their own journeys of self-discovery, opting instead for mimicry over mastery. We mistakenly believed that by imitating the words and actions of others, we would find enlightenment in our own experiences. When this did not occur, we dismissed those individuals as misguided or the teachings as flawed. In truth, we could not have been further from understanding.

It is true that the way is marked by the footsteps of those who have gone before us, without a doubt. Yet the markers to the way are much different than the way itself.

Markers possess the potential for alteration, manipulation, or relocation. The pathway is not subservient to the signage; rather, the signage is subordinate to its purpose of identification and description. This principle applies to our messengers and teachers, who are constrained by their own experiences and can only illuminate truths they are capable of articulating. Consequently, every sacred messenger has endured suffering, and their messages have often been distorted or misunderstood. They can guide us only to the extent that they affirm the existence of a path, rather than detailing its specifics. Our sacred texts remain mere words without the context of understanding. Even the most knowledgeable scholars face challenges in relating specific words or scriptures to our individual lives; their interpretations reflect their personal insights rather than universal truths. Nevertheless, it is essential for us to engage with each other's interpretations to gain a broader perspective of our world. However, it is equally vital that we explore the mysteries of existence independently, as it is our personal responsibility to attain self-knowledge and understand our connection to Allah and all creation. Failing to do so results in a cycle of the blind leading the blind, leading to conflict over who should guide the way.

So, why is it important to listen to one another while ultimately relying on our own understanding? At first glance, this approach may seem to foster intolerance and division. However, I contend that this is not the case. We often fail to provide one another with the opportunity to speak, preoccupied as we are with expressing our own views. We have yet to truly hear each other, remaining resistant to differing perspectives. Even in silence, our minds engage in constant debate, objecting to what we hear to reaffirm our beliefs. In safeguarding our convictions, we risk our own stagnation. We cannot comprehend what we do not know, particularly if we are unwilling to embrace new ideas. It is imperative that we learn to listen before dismissing unfamiliar information.

Our failure to listen stems from a fear-based reasoning system. We fear being misled by others, whom we often view as adversaries. This apprehension extends even to those we consider allies—individuals with whom we share similar beliefs. We perceive this group as close yet fundamentally separate, harboring an underlying distrust regarding their truths. This separation is rooted in our base nature, which encompasses a self-centered drive for personal survival. Our competition for survival has historically catalyzed evolution and progress, but it can only take us so far. Our obsessive focus on individual survival limits our collective achievements, stifling spiritual growth and preventing us from recognizing the needs of the whole. The masters, prophets, and enlightened individuals have transcended this limitation; they have come to understand that there is no distinction between themselves and others. Consequently, they dedicated their lives to the welfare and advancement of humanity. Upon realizing their connection to God and all creation, they recognized that individual survival is trivial in comparison to the greater good. This concept is exemplified in the story of Noah, peace be upon him, who, despite the impending destruction, sought to enlighten all and offer them salvation through the ark rather than prioritizing only his immediate family.

 Imagine being the very last person alive on the planet: then further imagine that no other form of life existed at all, and you were just waiting for death from starvation. The reality of that experience can hardly be imagined.

The mind will not allow the thought to persist for very long until it begins to grasp hopes of continued survival by some miraculous means. It won't allow it because deep within us we know that we cannot exist in a completely solitary state. We recognize that it would be impossible for us to exist without other forms of life, physically, emotionally, and spiritually. We cannot sustain ourselves without other life to, support, interact with, and to be a witness to our existence. This is a truth that none of us can deny, yet we walk amongst one another with complete disregard, not fully accepting the necessity of one other.

There is a common misunderstanding amongst spiritual seekers that each of us is Allah. We are not Allah. Allah, however, is each of us. There is a subtle and yet distinctive difference between these two thought forms. In the first instance, we take within ourselves the belief that we are greater than we are. In the other, we recognize that our individual insignificance is only made significant by the reality that Allah chooses to reside with us. We can never become or abide within Allah. We cannot perceive the unperceivable, yet that which we attempt to conceptualize can inhabit us. Before we are, Allah is. As we begin to understand this simple truth, our feet slowly yet assuredly start to find their place along the path.

So, what does that mean? What does it mean for Allah to be each of us? Does that mean Allah inhabits us, possesses us? Or does it mean that Allah exists within us? None of those are true. Does the breath inhabit you or possess you? No. The breath occurs with you and participates in your existence. The same is true with Allah. He is co-occurring in your experience: existing nearer to you than your jugular vein and witnessing your reality as both author and reader. This is the fundamental meaning of the name Al-Haqq, The Real, or the only reality. Allah is all that ultimately truly exists. Everything else can only ever be a fragment of His creation.

On the authority of Abu Hurayrah (may Allah be pleased with him), who said that the Messenger of Allah (peace be upon him) said:

Allah (mighty and sublime be He) will say on the Day of Resurrection: O son of Adam, I fell ill, and you visited Me not. He will say: O Lord, and how should I visit You when You are the Lord of the worlds? He will say: Did you not know that My servant So-and-so had fallen ill, and you did not visit him? Did you not know that had you visited him you would have found Me with him? O son of Adam, I asked you for food and you fed Me not. He will say: O Lord, and how should I feed You when You are the Lord of the worlds? He will say: Did you not know that My servant So-and-so asked you for food and you did not feed him? Did you not know that had you fed him you would surely have found that (the reward for doing so) with Me? O son of Adam, I asked you to give Me to drink and you did not give Me to drink. He will say: O Lord, how should I give You to drink when You are the Lord of the worlds? He will say: My servant So-and-so asked you to give him to drink and you did not give him to drink. Had you given him to drink you would have surely found that with Me.

~Hadith 18, 40 Hadith Qudsi, it was related by Imam Muslim.

There is only one way regardless of the tradition that may be followed, the way is The same. The way is acceptance of and submission to peace. Peace is the natural state of existence and is the foundation of all things. Peace is inertia at rest. Peace is the source.

Before creation, there exists only the stillness of peace, which is fundamentally our essence and the foundation of our being. It is only upon recognizing that peace is the path forward that we can begin to transform our reality from one driven by ego and chaos to one of enlightened contentment. This journey is echoed throughout history by every prophet, sage, teacher, guru, and guide. Spiritual masters form a unified brotherhood that conveys a singular message: the source of all creation stems from one origin, and our submission to that source is essential.

We enter this world with an inherent desire to embrace submission, yet we often find ourselves in turmoil when we deny this calling in favor of ego-driven desires. When enough individuals abandon this birthright, society descends into chaos, promoting fear, depression, anxiety, anger, and aggression as norms.

The solution lies in the exploration and discovery of the self, coupled with the acceptance of others who are on a similar journey. It is not our role to judge the hearts or intentions of those we encounter; only Allah can assess mankind and the contents of our hearts. It is neither necessary nor possible for us to fully understand one another, as the Bible teaches that Allah has confounded human language to thwart our arrogant pursuits of self-glorification. Our purpose is not to collectively attain friendship with Allah, but to individually engage in a struggle characterized by patience and consistency. This embodies the essence of submission—the path of self-discovery that connects us to the purpose of our creation.

We inhabit a world marred by an incessant pursuit of selfish desires. This perpetual state of self-adulation ensnares us in suffering. We mistakenly believe that fulfilling our desires will lead to happiness, that appeasing ourselves will bring contentment and peace. In truth, the opposite is the reality. Genuine happiness and peace arise only when we prioritize the needs of others above our own. True self-fulfillment is found in meeting the needs of others.

In Islamic tradition, it is taught that the Prophet Muhammad, peace be upon him, stated that the best among people are those who are most beneficial to others. Those who have learned to submit to the Almighty ultimately serve humanity, thereby becoming better individuals. They discover that their actual needs are far less than they once believed, making it easier to fulfill the needs of others. Such individuals find contentment and peace in simplicity, needing little beyond Allah.

Minimizing or abandoning egoic desire spans numerous traditions. It is a common ideology, despite it being pursued by few. We have been convinced in most societies that the pursuit of personal fulfillment and success is the golden ticket. We have been convinced that this dream is the basis of living a complete life. The prosperity doctrine is taught globally at this point, creating an epidemic of societally induced selfishness. We see this in popular idioms like "dog eat dog," "the American dream," or "pull yourself up by your bootstraps," and so on. There is a popular story of an individual who was given a view of both heaven and hell. In hell, the person saw that everyone was seated at a table with long spoons affixed to their arms. The spoons were so long that there was no way that they could ever feed themselves the wondrous meal that was placed before them, so they sat in misery, only able to behold the meal without ever partaking in its delicacy.

Following this, the same individual was taken to heaven, where they witnessed a similar scene: people seated at a table with long spoons affixed to their arms, with a magnificent meal laid before them. The notable difference was that the heavenly inhabitants were feeding one another, deriving joy from their shared experience. One group found happiness, contentment, and peace in serving each other, while the other remained mired in misery due to selfishness. This parable, recounted in various traditions, serves as a poignant reminder to prioritize the well-being of others over our own. It emphasizes the joy found in service and giving rather than merely receiving.

Despite the widespread acknowledgment of this parable, we continue to observe a world rife with corruption and self-serving behaviors. Why does this occur? How can such enduring wisdom exist and resonate with countless individuals yet remain unimplemented? We hear the teachings but often fail to internalize their meaning. We listen, yet the words seem to evaporate against our consciousness. Each of us tends to justify our actions, believing that our self-rationalization is validated by our material abundance. In our pride, we equate our possessions with moral righteousness, assuming that our achievements signal divine favor.

However, the material aspects of life are transient and ultimately serve as mere distractions, not indicators of spiritual progress. When we fulfill all our physical desires, we risk losing sight of our spiritual growth.

This is not to suggest that we must renounce the enjoyment of worldly life. On the contrary, we can fully embrace the richness of this existence, as intended by Allah. Yet, true enjoyment transforms when we take on the role of caretakers for one another and for all of creation. In such a paradigm, disparities in resources dissolve, and basic human needs are met. We no longer witness children suffering from hunger, women facing abuse, or elders being neglected. The suffering of animals and the degradation of the earth are stark reminders of our failure to extend our compassion beyond ourselves, leading to a loss of perspective on our collective responsibilities.

We have forsaken submission to a higher purpose in favor of self-idolatry, often sacrificing our souls for trivial gains. However, the path to rectifying these errors is remarkably simple. It takes only a moment to redirect the heart. By inclining ourselves toward peace, we take our first step onto the straight path—a journey that may not lead to any particular destination in this life but can be found in every corner of the earth.

Part II

The journal

This journal is designed to facilitate the implementation of a daily contemplation practice. Each day presents a question or statement for reflection. Aim to set aside 5 to 10 minutes in the morning, afternoon, and evening to ponder the day's prompt and record your insights.

The Tao teaches us that "the way that can be told is not the way." This wisdom elucidates why many individuals find traditional religions unfulfilling and inadequate in guiding their paths. Each messenger, prophet, or holy figure depicted in sacred texts conveys a message about how to exist, rather than prescribing a specific identity. This fundamental misconception often leads believers to become lost in their identities; we become preoccupied with what we think we are rather than unraveling the essence of simply being. Consequently, the core message becomes obscured, and the path forward is overlooked. The opportunity to discover this path exists in every moment and within each breath. Yet, we often neglect to pause and truly notice these moments, allowing our breath to go unnoticed.

Meditation is presented as a tool for self-discovery and for unraveling the mysteries of our existence. However, meditation is not merely an activity we engage in; it is a state that arises. As we embark on the practice of meditation, we are often confronted with a cacophony of thoughts clamoring for attention. It is common to feel that something is amiss or to perceive a failure. In our attempts to concentrate on our breath, we may find that our thoughts intensify. This reality stems from the brain's connection to our olfactory system, where each breath attempts to process information, triggering thoughts. True meditation occurs when we cultivate a meditative state, which requires first learning to listen to and fully resolve the thoughts that surface. This process is known as contemplation, and it helps the mind learn when to rest. When the mind is at rest, we enter a meditative state, which can ultimately lead us to discover our path.

As you navigate through this contemplation journal, keep in mind that the suggested prompts are merely guidelines. If a particular day's prompt does not resonate with you, feel free to set it aside and focus on the thoughts occupying your heart and mind. Should you wish to spend more than one day on a prompt, take the necessary time; it is your responsibility to progress at a pace that suits you. This seemingly self-centered endeavor of self-exploration is, in fact, the first step toward benefitting all of humanity.

There is no right or wrong approach to contemplation or meditation; each individual's journey is unique. Anyone claiming to know precisely what you need is misguided and may be more interested in elevating themselves than in genuinely guiding you.

There is a hadith, a traditional saying in Islam, which conveys that the Prophet Muhammad, may peace be upon him, taught that on the Day of Resurrection, individuals will be questioned about how they utilized the blessings bestowed upon them by Allah. One man will claim, "I studied religious knowledge and taught it for Your sake." In response, Allah will declare, "You have lied; you taught so that others would perceive you as knowledgeable." Consequently, this man will be condemned to be dragged along his face toward punishment in Hellfire.

This saying serves as a caution to those who have attained a level of spiritual insight, warning them against arrogance in their possession and dissemination of knowledge. It reminds students to recognize that not all teachers approach their roles with humility or with the pure intention of connecting others to Allah or facilitating their growth; in some cases, the motivation may stem from self-promotion and ego. Allah alone is Al-Haadi, The Guide, and Ar-Rasheed, The Infallible Teacher; there is no need for anyone else.

Let me clarify: I do not mean to imply that a teacher lacks merit or cannot contribute positively to one's spiritual journey. However, relying solely on a teacher can lead one astray. We are all human, none greater than another, and we are each susceptible to temptation and the inclination toward selfishness

(If a woman fears indifference or neglect from her husband, there is no blame on either of them if they seek ˈfairˈ settlement, which is best. Humans are ever inclined to selfishness. But if you are gracious and mindful ˈof Allahˈ, surely Allah is All-Aware of what you do.)

~Holy Quran 4:128

It is inherent in our nature to prioritize ourselves, and even the most pious among us can regress into base behaviors. Ultimately, Allah alone suffices. Humans, by their very nature, are flawed. It was never intended for us to place our hope in one another; we are meant to trust each other only through faith in Allah and to love one another by first learning to love Allah.

For trust and love to flourish, an act of submission is essential. How can we submit to that which is flawed if we are unable to submit to the perfection that is Allah? This principle has been established since the beginning of creation. Our failure to prioritize this submission has contributed to the chaos we observe in the world. From the outset, we see a tendency to submit to personal desires rather than to Allah. The act of submission represents an effort to abandon selfish inclinations in favor of recognizing that, by yielding our will to Allah, we commit ourselves to being beneficial to humanity. This transformation can only occur through introspection.

As we begin to understand ourselves, we will increasingly perceive the peace and mercy of Allah in our lives. This understanding will guide us toward the ability to submit to peace and extend mercy to one another. I pray that as you embark on your journey of discovery, your path is filled with tranquility.

We cannot truly know Allah without first understanding ourselves.

Reflection 1
What do you know to be real, indisputably real?

Reflection 2
What makes truth, Truth?

Reflection 3
Can the adverse of a truth also be true?

Reflection 4
You are here. What else do you need?

Reflection 5
What is time?

Reflection 6
What is life?

Reflection 7
What is breath?

Reflection 8
What is Death?

Reflection 9
What is love?

Reflection 10
What is Fear?

Reflection 11
Who am I?

Reflection 12
Can your reality be "True" when you are the only experiencer of it?

Reflection 13
Can an individual perception of truth ever really be true?

Reflection 14
Desire is?

Reflection 15
Without observation, does time exists?

Reflection 16
Given your understanding of life, what determines it's unfolding?

Reflection 17
What distinguishes breath from the experience of breath?

Reflection 18
Does death exist if you are unable to experience it?

Reflection 19
Allah?

Reflection 20
Fear and separation. So you're alone now what?

Reflection 21
Who are you in relation to who you think you are?

Reflection 22
If now is now, can it ever be missed?

Reflection 23
How does the rest of the world fit into your truth?

Reflection 24
How does your love include you?

Reflection 25
When is now?

Reflection 26
What governs your life?

Reflection 27
What exists without perception?

Day 28 What is silence?

Day 29 When are you, you?

Day 30 Does existence precede reality?

Reflection 31
What does "being" mean?

Reflection 32
What is meditation?

Reflection 33
What is enlightenment?

www.ingramcontent.com/pod-product-compliance
Lightning Source LLC
Chambersburg PA
CBHW081409130726
47998CB00011B/3124